The FIRST BOOK of
THE HUMAN SENSES

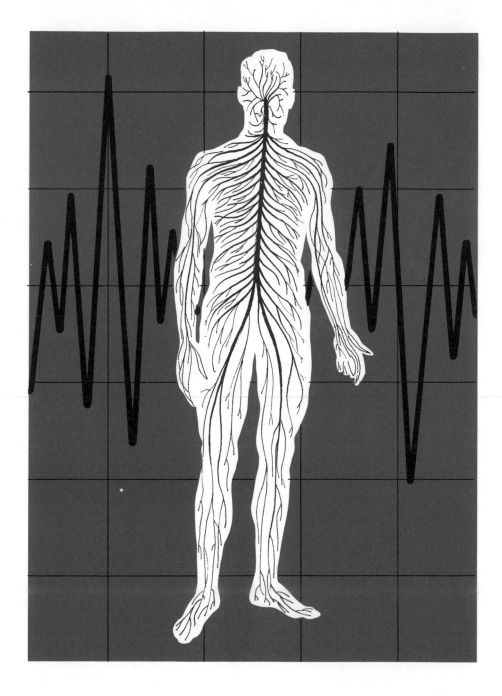

The FIRST BOOK of

THE HUMAN SENSES

by Gene Liberty

Pictures by Robert Tidd

Franklin Watts, Inc.
575 Lexington Avenue • New York 22

For my other family
THE LUMS

SBN 531-00555-0

6   7   8   9   10
Library of Congress Catalog Card Number: 61-7499
Copyright © 1961 by Franklin Watts, Inc.
Printed in the United States of America

Contents

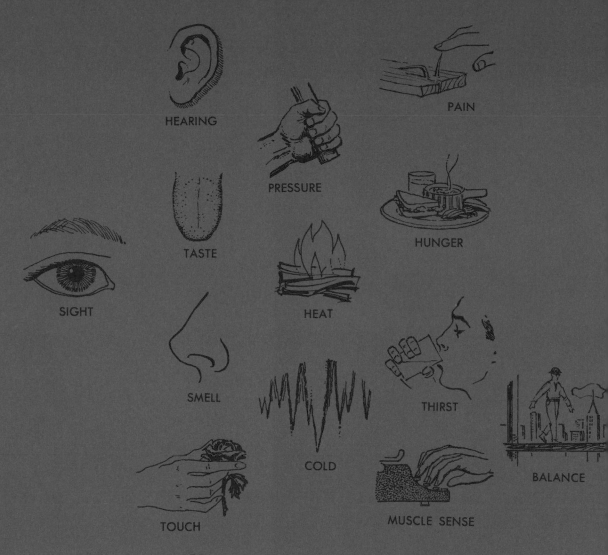

HEARING

PAIN

PRESSURE

TASTE

HUNGER

SIGHT

HEAT

SMELL

THIRST

COLD

MUSCLE SENSE

BALANCE

TOUCH

How Many Senses Do We Have?

Our knowledge of the human senses is growing. In past years we thought that we had only five senses: *sight, hearing, taste, smell,* and *touch.* As we gain deeper wisdom about our bodies, we are learning that there are many more human senses than the original five.

We now know, for example, that touch is one of a group of senses called the *feeling senses.* The other feeling senses are *pressure, heat, cold,* and *pain.* In addition we recognize today that *hunger, thirst, muscle sense,* and *balance* are separate senses.

Our present list of senses, shown above, has grown to thirteen. The list should grow still larger as we discover more about ourselves.

GENE LIBERTY

THE SENSES IN A WORLD OF CHANGE

THE HUMAN SENSES create for each of us a remarkable map of life. Sight, hearing, taste, smell, feeling, and the other senses are like compasses which help us to explore the world. They point to what is happening inside and outside our bodies. Through them we learn how everything within us and around us changes continuously.

Listen. What sounds do you hear? Perhaps voices in the next room become louder, or the honk of an automobile horn fades, or a piano starts to play. These sounds disappear just as quickly as they are heard and are immediately replaced by others.

Smell the air. Here, too, you will experience change. For example, food odors from the kitchen may mix interestingly with new odors carried into the house by a breeze. A list of the different odors you smell in a single day would show great variety. Food, smoke, the ocean, gasoline, garbage, animals, perfume, flowers, soap, the human body, wax, and freshly cut grass produce just a few of the everyday odors familiar to our sense of smell.

Look around you. Outdoors you may see great activity. In the room where you are reading, the strongest movement seen by your eyes might be the rise and fall of your chest as you breathe.

Are you thirsty? Perhaps not at this moment, but change is a great rule of nature that directs and informs our senses. Over a period of time your mouth and throat naturally dry out. Later your sense of thirst will tell you when your body requires more water.

1

ELECTRICITY AND UNDERSTANDING

THE SENSES constantly report to the brain on experiences like those just discussed. Here is what takes place:

First, a particular *sense organ*, such as the ear, the eye, or the nose is stimulated. *Organs* are parts of the body that perform special jobs. A *stimulus* is anything that causes the sense organs to perform some activity. Sound that reaches our ears, light that enters our eyes, and smells that are breathed through our noses are all stimuli.

After the sense organ is stimulated, it sends a message to the brain. The sense organ changes the message from its original form — say, sound waves produced by a bell, or the odor of a flower — into short bursts of electricity, called *impulses*. The impulses, which are really an electrical code for the message, travel along the nerves connecting the sense organ to the brain.

In the brain, the coded message of electrical impulses is decoded. Although the sense organ receives the stimulus, it is the brain that *perceives*, or understands, what the stimulus means. Thus our ears receive sound waves, but the brain perceives that we are listening to the cry of a bird, the thump of a drum, or the voice of a friend.

WHEN YOU ACT WITHOUT THINKING

SOMETIMES the sense organs stimulate muscles to act even before the brain knows what is happening. Such *reflexes* frequently occur when you are in danger. For example, if you touch a hot object, your hand automatically jerks back. The heat causes a message to flash from the nerves in your skin to the spinal cord, a cable located in the backbone that is made up of millions of nerves. The message then speeds to the muscles of your hand, directing them to contract and pull away. Another message, sent up through the spinal cord, informs your brain that your hand has touched something hot.

A different type of reflex — one in which the brain receives no information — also takes place in our bodies. An example is the change in size of the pupils of the eyes to allow more or less light to enter. In a dark room the pupils are large, but in a bright room they become smaller. Although the muscles that control this movement are very active, they do their work without ever sending messages to the brain.

When you are hungry and you see or smell food, a similar reflex occurs. Saliva starts to flow in your mouth. The saliva softens the food and wets it to slide smoothly down your throat. At the same time, gastric juices flow in the stomach. The gastric juices help to digest and break down food so that it can be absorbed or eliminated by the body. The flow of saliva and gastric juices, like the change in size of the pupils of the eyes, is a reflex that occurs without the brain receiving information.

Do Our Senses
Always Tell the Truth?

At times our senses deceive us or become tired. Strong odors, which seem overpowering when we first smell them, soon become milder and then practically disappear because the nose fatigues quickly. Delicate tastes vanish as we continue to eat and the tongue becomes accustomed to them. After reading for a length of time, some people find that their eyes are weary and unable to see clearly. Sounds often seem to come from a confusing direction. Many iced drinks lose much of their flavor because cold dulls our ability to taste. Our sense of balance occasionally deserts us and we fall. A color-blind person may see the same color when he looks at a red rose or a gray rock.

These are tricks that the senses play on the mind. But the mind is not always the victim, for it frequently misleads the senses.

A speeding car skids and crashes into a parked car near a street corner. On the sidewalk two men are facing in the direction of the crash. If both men had photographed the accident, they would have gotten almost identical pictures. Yet when the men described what they had seen, their stories were very different.

A boy is playing the violin at a party. All of the guests seem to be suffering because the young player is producing too many screeching sounds. His parents, however, listen with pleased and appreciative expressions on their faces.

An artist overhears a group of people discussing his painting. Half of the people like the painting. It is only their remarks that the artist remembers.

These three stories illustrate how messages from our senses can be changed by our feelings and the state of our minds. One of the witnesses developed fear when he heard the two cars crash. The other was daydreaming and became confused. Thus their stories were influenced by what they felt. Mom and Pop were listening to their son with love rather than their ears. Even the disturbing screeches of the bow sounded like music to them. And the artist heard only what he wanted to hear about his work.

If the senses are capable of fooling the mind, and the mind in turn is capable of fooling the senses — what are we to believe? The answer is that we can best rely on our senses and our minds when we learn how they work and what they are capable of truly or falsely telling us. Such knowledge reveals us to ourselves. Further, it gives us an opportunity to understand a part of the exciting puzzle of human nature.

How the Nerves Work

THE HUMAN BODY contains billions of nerves which serve the senses as wires for carrying messages. Over twelve billion nerves are contained in the brain alone. Some of these nerves are surprisingly long, extending to three feet or more. Others have lengths measured in fractions of an inch.

The thicker a nerve is, the faster it transmits messages. In the thickest nerves, messages travel at nearly 200 miles per hour, about three times faster than the top speed permitted a car on superhighways.

The Parts of a Nerve Cell

IF YOU look at a nerve cell, or *neuron*, under a microscope, you will see a blob with one or more tiny threads coming out of it. The blob is the *cell body*, which is the control center, or headquarters, of the nerve. As you can see in the diagram on this page, nerves also have entrances and exits. Messages enter a nerve through the *dendrites* (shorter threads) and leave by the *axon* (the longest thread). Some axons are so thin that if 6,000 of them were placed one on top of the other, they would only reach a height of one-quarter of an inch.

Motor Nerve

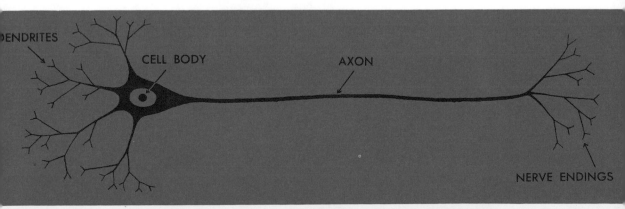

DENDRITES

CELL BODY

AXON

NERVE ENDINGS

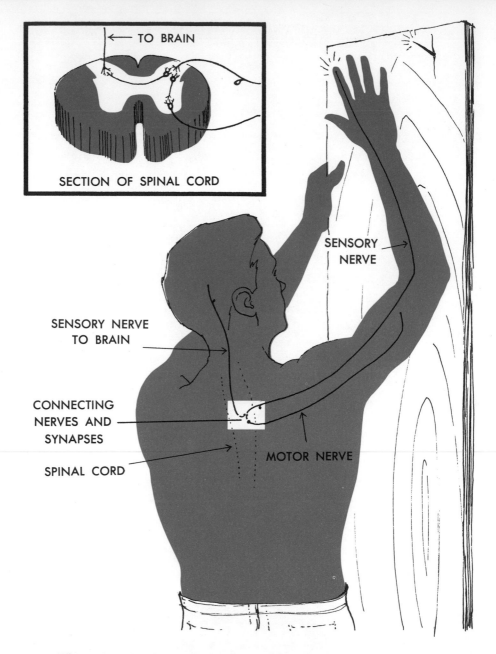

TO BRAIN

SECTION OF SPINAL CORD

SENSORY
NERVE

SENSORY NERVE
TO BRAIN

CONNECTING
NERVES AND
SYNAPSES

MOTOR NERVE

SPINAL CORD

The pointed nail causes a reflex to take place. Before the brain
knows what is happening, the hand has already pulled away.

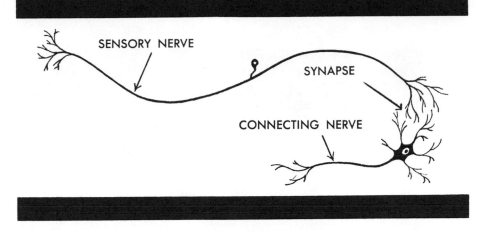

SENSORY NERVE

SYNAPSE

CONNECTING NERVE

The Different Nerves
and What They Do

THERE ARE three kinds of nerves, each with a special job to perform:

Sensory nerves send messages to the brain or to the spinal cord about what is happening inside and outside the body.

Connecting nerves act as bridges, carrying messages to and from other nerves.

Motor nerves deliver orders from the brain and spinal cord to different parts of the body, such as the muscles, telling them what to do.

To understand how the three kinds of nerves work together, imagine that your finger has accidentally touched the point of a sharp nail. A message immediately flashes from the dendrites of the sensory nerve, which are buried in the skin, through the cell body. As we have seen, the message is actually a group of short electrical impulses. From the cell body the message, in the form of these impulses, travels along the axon and into the spinal cord. The arrows

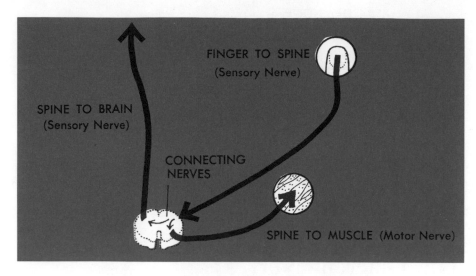

FINGER TO SPINE
(Sensory Nerve)

SPINE TO BRAIN
(Sensory Nerve)

CONNECTING
NERVES

SPINE TO MUSCLE (Motor Nerve)

Path of a Reflex

in the picture above show the path that the message takes.

When the message reaches the end of the axon, it crosses a *synapse* and enters the dendrites of the connecting nerve. The synapse is a region containing chemical fluids which transmit nerve messages. In a way, we could say that the message swims through the synapse, for the ends of the axon of the sensory nerve do not actually touch the dendrites of the connecting nerve.

After the message passes through the connecting nerve, it crosses another synapse and enters the dendrites of a motor nerve. In the meantime, a different sensory nerve in the spinal cord informs the brain that the finger has touched a sharp object.

But a reflex is taking place! The message speeding along the motor nerve to your finger muscle travels faster than the message to your brain. You will pull back your finger a fraction of a second before your brain understands why you are acting so quickly.

8

We read using light that is reflected from the page to our eyes.

SEEING

VISION is the keenest and most important of all the human senses. For with our eyes we capture the colors and patterns, shapes and shadows, much of the beauty and ugliness, and movement and stillness that surround us.

When we are awake our eyes rarely rest. They are remarkably strong and quick. "Eyes are as bold as lions," said the writer Ralph Waldo Emerson, "roving, running, leaping, here and there, far and near." In a few short seconds, our eyes can read a line of printed words, look at a painting, and pick out a star — all without great effort or strain.

Figure 1: Light Travels in Straight Lines

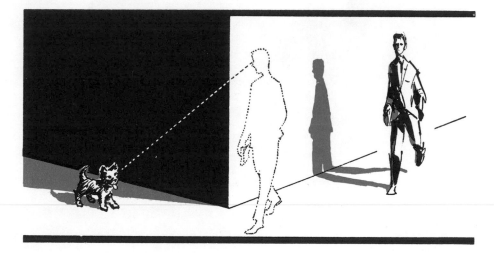

Light and Lenses

WE SEE objects only when light from them enters our eyes. Those objects that give off their own light, such as the sun, electric light bulbs, and candles, are known as *luminous*. Most objects that we see, however, are *illuminated*; that is, they reflect, or bounce back, light to our eyes. Examples of illuminated objects are people, the sky, trees, walls, books, clothing, and furniture. The moon, too, is illuminated, for it is seen by the light it reflects from the sun.

Light normally travels in straight lines, which is why we cannot see around a corner. In Figure 1, the man cannot see the dog until he reaches the position shown by the dotted lines.

Light bends only when it passes from one substance, such as air, into another substance, such as water or glass. It is the bending of light, or *refraction* (*see* Figure 2), that causes a fish in water to appear in a different position than it really is; makes a spoon seemingly twist as it enters a bowl of soup; and allows lenses to form clear images.

Figure 2: Light Bends When It Travels from Air into Other Substances

The real position of the fish is shown on the left. We see it, however, in the position shown on the right. The spoon appears to bend at the surface of the water. When we look through a window, we see fairly accurate images because the window glass bends the light only slightly.

11

A *lens* is a curved piece of glass or other transparent material that bends light rays passing through it. *Convex* lenses cause the light rays to come together, and *concave* lenses cause them to spread apart. Lenses control and bend the light that enters eyeglasses, microscopes, magnifying glasses, telescopes, cameras, and the human eye.

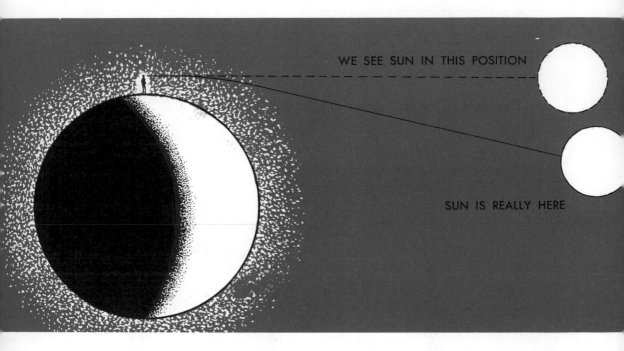

WE SEE SUN IN THIS POSITION

SUN IS REALLY HERE

The sun's rays bend when they enter the earth's atmosphere from outer space. Thus in the morning we see the sun before it actually rises over the horizon. After the sun has actually set, we continue to receive its light for a short while. The bending of the sun's rays — in the morning and the evening — gives us a longer day.

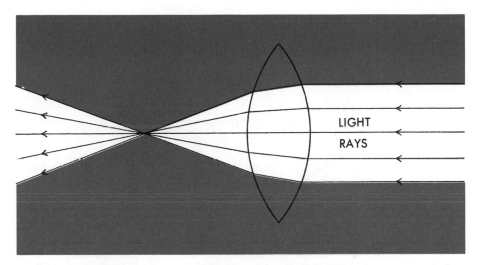

A Convex Lens Brings Light Together

A Concave Lens Spreads Light Apart

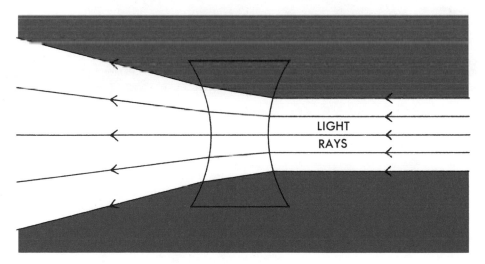

Figure 3: Convex Lenses Form Images That Are Upside Down

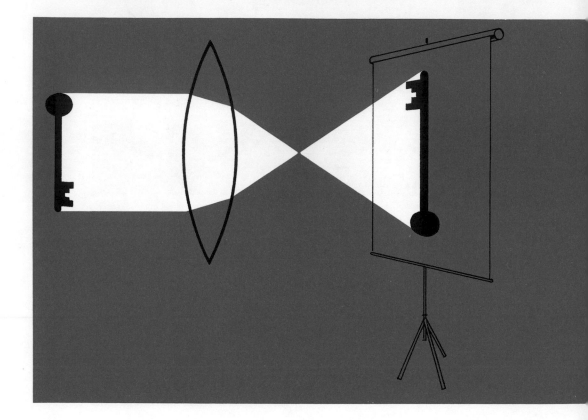

Guardians of the Eye

OUR EYES are complicated and delicate sense organs. They are remarkable in design, fascinating in the way they work, and strong in their defenses against injury.

Sitting in two hollow pockets in the skull, the eyes are protected by the bones that surround them. The eyelids serve as fast moving doors which can shut in a wink to keep out threatening objects. A soft pad of fat cushions the eyes from damage by shock. Perspiration and dust are largely stopped from entering the eyes by two sets of protective screens made of hair — the eyebrows and the eyelids.

And what of tears? This watery solution, which we usually think of as demonstrating pain or grief, has vital importance in the health of our eyes.

Tears are produced by the tear, or *lachrymal*, glands. There are two tear glands over each eye, behind the upper eyelid. When you blink, the tears spread over the cornea of the eyes (*see* Figure 4) in a thin film. They keep the cornea clean and moist and wash away dust, bacteria, soot, and other invading irritants. Although we can blink when we choose to, we hardly notice that blinking is mostly automatic. This regular opening and closing of the lids cleans and protects our eyes without our thinking about it.

The Window and the Curtain

THE *cornea* is the window of the eye. Tough and clear, the cornea shields the eye from injury and permits light rays to pass through. It also acts as a magnifying glass, enlarging the images carried by the light rays.

Behind the cornea lies a small chamber filled with the *aqueous humor*, a fluid that is a weak solution of salt in water. This chamber, like the larger chamber filled with the *vitreous humor* (*see* Figure 4), helps the eye to maintain its round shape. The vitreous

15

Figure 4: The Human Eye

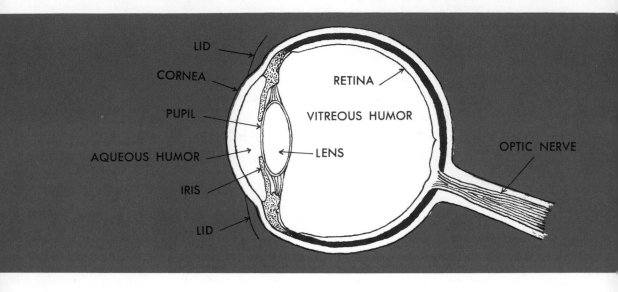

humor is a thick fluid having the appearance of a clear jelly.

Look at your eyes in the mirror, and you will see that each has a colored ring with a black hole in the center. The ring is the *iris*, a muscle that acts like a curtain, opening and closing to allow more or less light into the eye. The hole is the *pupil*, the entrance through which all light passes.

When we talk of the color of a person's eyes, we are describing the irises. Most frequently they are a shade of brown, blue, or green. At night the irises open wide, so that all available light may enter the eyes. On a sunny day the reverse happens: the irises close down to prevent us from being blinded by the brightness of the sun.

16

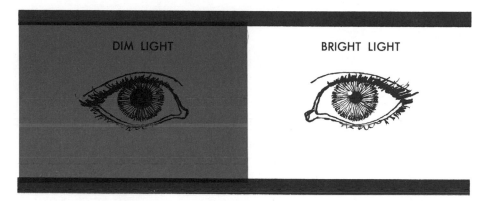

DIM LIGHT

BRIGHT LIGHT

In bright light, the iris closes over the pupil, making it smaller. When the light is dim, however, the iris opens and the pupil becomes wider, permitting more light to enter the eye.

The Lens and the Screen

LOCATED just behind the iris is perhaps the most wonderful part of the human eye — a transparent convex *lens* that is capable of changing its shape.

The eye lens, working like the glass lens in Figure 3, bends the light rays that pass through it and focuses them on the *retina*, located at the back of the eye. *Focusing* is the ability to form sharp, clear images. Unlike the glass lens, however, the eye lens adjusts its shape to meet different focusing situations.

When you are looking at a distant object, the eye lens becomes thin and long, like a sausage. It will become thicker and shorter and bulge in the middle — much like a football with flattened ends — if the object is close.

To see how the eye lens changes focus, close one eye and stare at a chair at the far end of the room. Then hold a pencil straight up about fifteen inches in front of your open eye. Keep staring at the chair. You will notice that the pencil appears blurred. Shift your attention from the chair to the pencil. Now it is the chair that is blurred and the pencil that is clear.

In shifting from the chair to the pencil, the eye lens quickly changed from a thin shape to a thick shape. If you were to look back at the chair, the eye lens would again become thin. Such changes in the eye lens are automatic. They occur constantly throughout the day. The eye lens bulges or thins out every time we look at something and then look at another thing that is closer or further away.

When the eye lens changes its shape, it is doing the work you do by hand when you operate a movie or slide projector. The lens of the projector is moved back and forth until a sharp image is projected on the screen. The lengthening and shortening of the eye lens has a similar purpose — to project sharp images on the retina, which is the screen of the eye. As shown in Figure 4, the retina covers the rear wall of the eyeball.

Because the eye lens is convex (*see* Figure 5), the images received by the retina are upside down. The whole world is topsy-turvy on the retina, much the same as a photograph viewed wrong-side-up. The brain, however, reverses the image on the retina, so that we see everything in its correct position — right-side-up!

Located in the retina are millions of *rods* and *cones*. These tiny nerve endings are sensitive to light and color. They send their messages to the brain through the *optic nerve*. The messages sent by the rods are different than those sent by the cones. Each has a special job to perform, generally depending on the time of the day.

The rods work only in dim light. They are blinded by bright light and are therefore used mostly for night vision. The rods also cannot tell colors apart in any light, either bright or dim. When the

18

Figure 5: The Convex Lens of the Eye Projects an Upside Down Image on the Retina

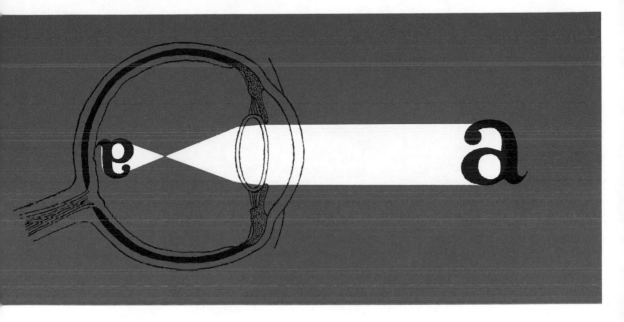

light is dim, the rods enable us to see different shapes, but the recognition of color is beyond their power. For this reason, colors that are easily identified during daytime appear to us at night as different shades of gray.

The cones are for daytime vision. Under sunlight or bright artificial light, they are sensitive to shapes and all the shades of all the colors. In dim light, when the rods work best, the cones do not work at all. If you were to look at an apple tree in the daytime, the cones in your eyes would send messages to your brain about the browns in the trunk and branches, the greens in the leaves, and the reds, greens, and yellows in the apples. In moonlight, which is about 150,000 times weaker than sunlight, the rods take over and the colors of the tree would not be visible. Instead of browns, greens, reds, and yellows, you would see glowing shades of silver gray.

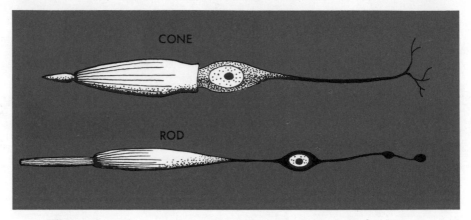

The rods and cones, located in the retina, send their messages of light and color via the optic nerve to the brain.

The Colors in White Light

THE WHITE light that we receive from the sun is really a rainbow-like mixture of colors. Some three hundred years ago, the English scientist Isaac Newton showed how these colors are produced when white light is broken up by a triangular glass *prism* (*see* Figure 6).

Newton passed a narrow beam of sunlight through one side of the prism. The light that came out the other side was allowed to fall on a wall across the room. He discovered that the prism spread the light, splitting it into a brilliant band of colors. That morning in 1666 was one of the rare moments in science when a mystery of nature is revealed to one man. For splashed onto the wall of New-ton's room was the formula of white light: a mixture of red, orange,

20

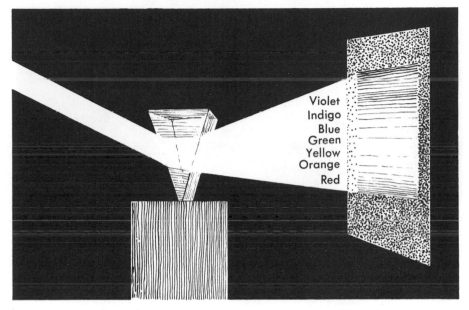

Violet
Indigo
Blue
Green
Yellow
Orange
Red

yellow, green, blue, indigo (dark blue-violet), and violet colors.

The band of colors hidden in white light held the solution to a question that inquisitive men had asked for thousands of years: What makes an object green, blue, red, or any other color? Newton's work showed that when white light falls on grass, for example, all of the colors contained in the light except green are *absorbed*, or taken up, by the grass. The eye sees only green colored light that is *reflected* — bounced back — by the grass. Other objects are seen in the same manner. They absorb the light of certain colors and reflect the light of one or more other colors. It is the reflected light that we see and recognize as the blue in a vase, the red-orange in a brick, the yellow in a banana, and so on.

21

Here are some further examples that show how colors are reflected or absorbed — or sometimes even disappear:

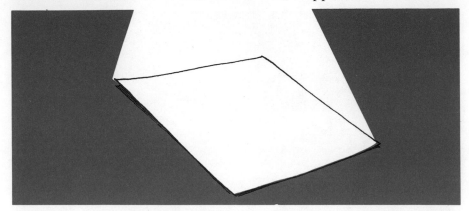

White light falls on white paper: A white object reflects all colors of light. None of the colors are absorbed, and you see the paper as white.

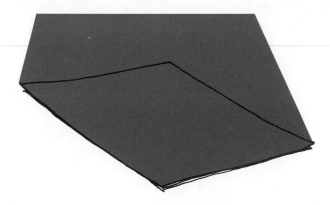

Red light falls on white paper: Since white objects reflect all colors, you see the paper as red. You would see the paper as violet or yellow if these or other colors were used instead of the red.

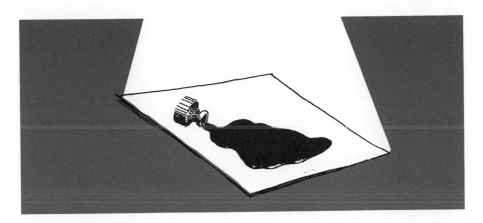

White light falls on black ink: Black objects absorb all colors, and you see the ink as black. What we call black is not considered to be a color since it is produced by the absence of all light and color.

White light falls on a red wall: You see the wall as red. The wall absorbs all the color in the light except red, which it reflects to your eyes.

Red light falls on a yellow wall: You see the wall as black since the wall absorbs all colors except yellow.

How Colors Affect People

WE THINK of colors, for the most part, as bringing beauty to our lives. For this reason we frequently overlook the importance of our sense of color in influencing our feelings, our moods, and our overall state of mind. By exciting or dulling our imaginations, irritating or pleasing us, making us feel hotter or cooler, gayer or sadder, colors contribute to many of the qualities that make up the human personality.

Take red. It is the color of life, suggesting warmth and strength and energy. Large amounts of red appear to be so strong that they are often difficult to live with. If red is mixed with yellow, orange — the tropical color of gaiety and excitement — is produced. Yellow itself is the color of sunshine and is cheerful, light, and airy.

Purple (or violet), unlike yellow, is quiet and serious, the color of wealth, ceremony, and importance. It is made by combining blue with red.

Blue is perhaps the most polite of colors — cool and distant and sometimes as far away, yet as attractive, as the sky. A mixture of blue and yellow results in green, a color that brings to mind the country in the summer and much that is peaceful and restful. Cool greens are made by using more blue than yellow. If more yellow is used, the green warms up, resembling the color of grass and leaves.

Brown, the natural color of wood, is another country color. It expresses sturdy growth and, for many people, a feeling of hospitality and friendship.

HEARING

SOUND reaches our ears like waves striking a coastline. Traveling through the sea of air we live in are quiet ripples and gentle rollers,

Figure 7: The Same Sound Wave Pictured Two Different Ways

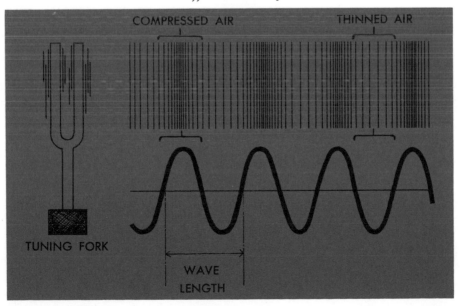

COMPRESSED AIR   THINNED AIR

TUNING FORK

WAVE LENGTH

choppy whitecaps and sharp breakers, towering combers and mighty swells — invisible waves of sound as varied in form as the surface of the sea itself.

The picture we use to illustrate the characteristics of sound waves indeed resembles the waves of the sea. It is shown in Figure 7.

The Motion of Sound

SOUNDS are produced by objects that *vibrate*, or move back and forth. Every sound that we hear — the human voice, thunder, a creaky floor, music, footsteps, bells, a knock on the door, a saw cutting wood, rain — is caused by vibrations.

The number of vibrations an object makes per second is called its *frequency*. Most people can hear sounds with frequencies between 16 and 20,000 vibrations per second. Sounds with frequencies below 16 vibrations per second are generally too low to hear; those with frequencies above 20,000 vibrations per second are too high.

Pitch, Loudness, and Quality

THE HIGHNESS or lowness of a sound describes its *pitch*. When a sound has a high pitch, like that of a whistle, it also has a high frequency; that is, the number of vibrations per second is great. The strings of a bass fiddle, on the other hand, vibrate slowly. They produce sound with a low pitch and a low frequency.

What happens to the pitch of a sound produced by striking the same key on a piano a number of times? The pitch of the sound, which is controlled by the number of vibrations per second, remains

Figure 8: Loud and Soft Sounds

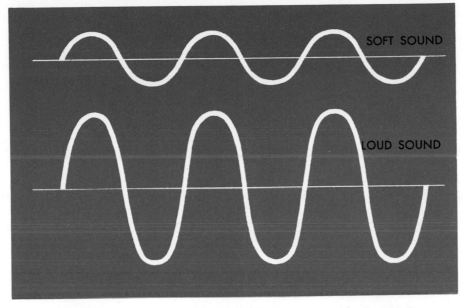

SOFT SOUND

LOUD SOUND

Loudness depends on the height of the sound wave, which shows how hard the air is squeezed together and how much it is thinned out.

the same each time the key is struck. However, the *loudness* of the sound may vary. Loudness depends on the strength, or size, of the vibrations, as shown in Figure 8. If you struck the key vigorously, the sound might be clearly heard by a listener standing one hundred feet away. A light tap would produce a sound that died out long before it reached him. Figure 10 shows two sounds which have the same pitch but differ in loudness.

In addition to pitch and loudness, sounds are also recognized by their *quality*. It is quality that permits us to distinguish between a musical note produced by a violin, a saxophone, other instruments, or the human voice. Although each of these notes may have identical pitch and loudness, their individual qualities make it easy to tell them apart.

27

Most vibrating objects produce a main, or most important, frequency plus some extra frequencies. The extra frequencies, called *overtones*, vibrate more rapidly than the main frequency. Overtones enrich the quality of the main frequency, making it mellow, fuller, and more pleasant to listen to.

How Sound Travels

THE SPEED of sound in air is about 700 miles per hour, or about 1100

Figure 9: Sounds of High and Low Pitch

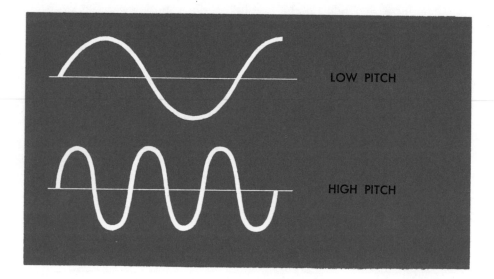

Pitch depends on frequency, which is the number of vibrations per second.

Figure 10: Loudness and Pitch Do Not Depend on Each Other

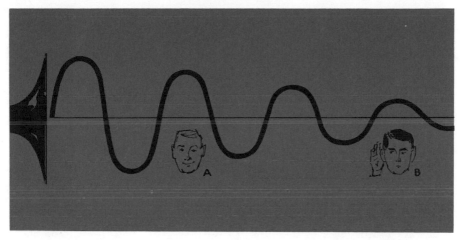

Sound loses strength as it gets further away from the vibrating body that produces it. Man A hears the sound of the trumpet more loudly than Man B. Both men, however, hear the same pitch, for the frequency (number of vibrations per second) remains unchanged.

feet per second. Although sound does travel in other substances, such as wood, water, and steel, it is air that carries to us the daily sounds of life.

We can see how sound waves are formed and how they travel in air if we follow what happens when we strike a tuning fork and start it vibrating. A tuning fork is a U-shaped piece of metal with a handle on the bottom. It produces sound of a fixed pitch and is used for tuning musical instruments. *See* Figure 7.

As the prongs move in one direction, they *compress*, or push together, the particles of air next to them. These particles pass the push along to a second group of particles, then to a third group, to a fourth group, a fifth, a sixth, and so on, as it continues to spread.

The prongs, which are vibrating, will complete their original swing and start to move back. When this happens, they create an empty space behind them. The air rushes to fill in the space, and all the particles that had been compressed now thin out.

Back and forth go the prongs, sending sound waves — groups of squeezed and thinned-out air particles — to your ear.

Inside the Ear

THE MOST important parts of the human ear are never seen. They are hidden inside the head. There, protected from injury, are the delicate *middle* and *inner ears*, which are responsible for our sense of hearing.

The part of the ear we see — the *outer ear* — catches sound waves and sends them along the ear, or *auditory*, canal. At the other end of the canal is the eardrum, or *tympanic membrane*, a thin, tightly stretched layer of skin that separates the outer and middle ears.

Sound waves cause the eardrum to vibrate. On the other side of the eardrum, in the middle ear, three tiny bones pick up the vibrations and transmit them to the inner ear. Because of their shapes, these bones are known as the *hammer*, the *anvil*, and the *stirrup*.

The lower section of the inner ear contains the *cochlea*. Made of bone and shaped like a snail, the cochlea is filled with a liquid, and is lined with thousands of tiny nerve endings. Sound waves pass through the outer and middle ears to the liquid, which begins to vibrate. The nerve endings are stimulated by the vibrating liquid.

Acting like the rods and cones in the eyes (which are sensitive to light), the nerve endings (which are sensitive to sound vibrations) send electrical impulses to the brain along the *auditory nerve*. The brain translates these impulses into the sensation we call sound.

Figure 11: The Human Ear

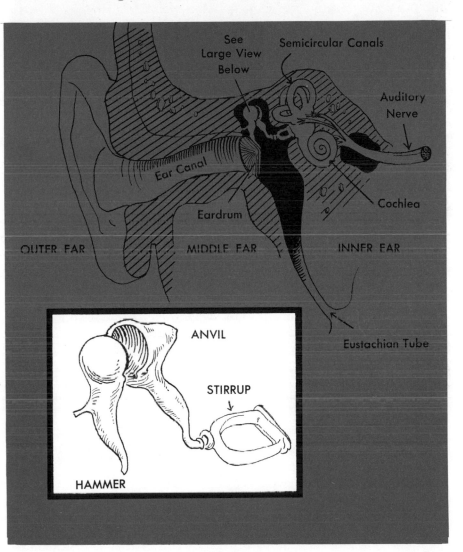

31

When we experience a sudden change in air pressure, as in a fast rising elevator, our eardrums feel uncomfortable. The middle ear carries with it the heavier air of the lower floors. At the higher floors, the air is lighter and exerts less pressure. The eardrum is pushed outward by the greater pressure in the middle ear, causing discomfort.

By opening your mouth and swallowing, this discomfort can be mostly eliminated. Swallowing forces the lighter air into the middle ear. The air travels through the Eustachian tube, which you see in Figure 11. The Eustachian tube is a passageway that permits air to enter the middle ear in order to keep the air pressure equal on both sides of the eardrum.

CHEMICAL SENSES – TASTE AND SMELL

AFTER a blindfold was placed over his eyes, the young man said he was ready for the experiment. The research scientists, whom he had volunteered to help, placed a clamp on his nose. Then they gave him a small amount of food to eat. He was told that it was a sliced apple. When he finished eating, the young man was startled to learn

from the scientists that they had fooled him. The apple was really a raw potato.

A few minutes later he made a similar mistake. This time the pear he thought he was eating turned out to be an onion.

The young man did not know what he was eating because the clamp on his nose prevented him from smelling. For although tasting and smelling are separate senses, they work together when we eat. Most frequently both senses are necessary in helping us to recognize different food flavors.

You can learn how your tongue and nose rely on each other by trying the same experiment: Cut an apple and a potato into small pieces. Have a friend place different pieces in your mouth without telling you what they are. Your eyes should be shut and your nose held closed with your fingers.

Are you eating apple or potato? With your sense of smell blocked, you will find it difficult to tell the two apart. If you release your fingers from your nose, however, each will have a familiar flavor that you can quickly identify.

The Third Eating Sense — Feeling

THE PLEASURE of eating depends on feeling foods as well as tasting and smelling them. Suppose for a moment that we could not feel with our tongues and mouths. If we were only able to taste and smell food, then part of the appeal of savoring a crackly potato chip, a smooth gob of whipped cream, or a juicy hamburger would be lost. All three senses — taste, smell and feel — work together to bring us full satisfaction and flavor from food.

The Human Laboratory

MAN'S NOSE and tongue are like instruments in an unusual chemical laboratory. Their job is to analyze, or recognize, the many different chemicals that are responsible for tastes and smells.

The chemicals we taste in foods are in dissolved form; that is, they are liquids. We cannot taste solids.

Here is a simple test to show how solids can be tasted only after they are dissolved in a liquid. Dry the top of your tongue with a towel. Then place some sugar at the very tip of your tongue. You will not be able to taste the sugar while your tongue remains dry. When your saliva flows, the sugar will dissolve and produce its familiar sweet taste.

Just as we cannot taste solids, we cannot smell either solids or liquids. We can only smell gases, which are usually dissolved in the air.

When a liquid is left standing or is heated, it changes into a gas. This process, called *evaporation*, creates many of the odors we know. The smells of soup, gasoline, perspiration, fresh paint, and flowers are all evaporation odors.

34

Bacteria cause a great number of odors, especially in foods. Both solid and liquid foods, which are spoiled by bacteria, almost always smell bad because of the gases produced by these tiny organisms.

Some solids, such as camphor, behave like liquids: on standing they turn into gases with strong odors. Other solids give off odors when they are destroyed by heat or fire. Typical odors of this kind are burning wood, rubber automobile tires that become heated in the summer, and candle smoke.

Familiar Odors Caused by Evaporation

Four Tastes Without Odors

THERE ARE four simple tastes that can be detected by the tongue without the help of the sense of smell. They are *bitter*, *sweet*, *sour*, and *salt*. Unlike the varied tastes of meats, vegetables, fruits, and many other foods, these four tastes can be detected by the tongue without the help of the sense of smell.

35

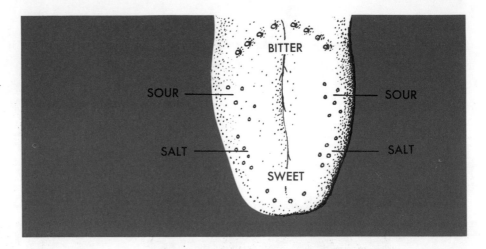

Taste Map of the Tongue

Each of these four tastes have special places on the tongue where they are felt most strongly. If you look at the taste map you will see that a bitter solution, for example, very strong tea, is best tasted at the back of the tongue. Up at the tip, the sweetness of sugar is most easily sensed. Sour solutions, such as vinegar or lemon juice, receive their strongest response from the tongue along its edges, about halfway back from the tip. And the saltiness of salt has its greatest strength along the edges just back of the sweet zone.

Taste That Is Switched On

AN UNCOMMON and unusual taste is that of electricity. When a very small electric current is applied to the tongue, different tastes can be produced. These tastes are sour or bitter or soapy, depending on the type of current used and its strength. Because of the possibility of injury, this experiment should not be tried at home.

Taste and the Bumps on Your Tongue

IF YOU look at the top of your tongue in a mirror, you will see that it is covered with tiny bumps. The smaller bumps are located at the front of the tongue, the bigger ones at the back. Within each bump are *taste buds*, which house the sensory nerves of taste. Your tongue contains about 9000 taste buds. The actual tasting is done by the sensory nerves. They are similar to the one on page 7.

Each sensory nerve has a fine tip at its end. The tip extends through the taste bud and reaches the surface of the tongue. When you eat, the chemicals in the food touch the tips and stimulate them. A message instantly passes from the tips through the cells along the nerve fiber and into the brain. There the taste of the food is combined with its aroma and its feeling to create the over-all sensation of flavor.

Taste Among Animals

HUMANS can taste suprisingly small bits of food chemicals. Yet some members of the animal world outdo us in taste sensitivity. Scientists report that the least amount of sugar we can taste is still 135 times greater than that required by the admiral butterfly. The minnow, a small fish of the carp family, can detect 500 times less sugar than we can. And the common housefly will be attracted to a sugar solution that is 1500 times too weak for us to taste.

The comparison between human taste and animal taste, however, is not all one-sided. Some animals cannot experience all of the tastes we do. Cats, for example, are unable to taste the sweetness of sugar. Because birds have few taste buds, many of them do not seem to rely on their taste sense while eating. They often eat extremely bitter seeds without any visible objection. Toads, too, lack the ability to identify bitterness. Together with a number of their amphibian cousins, they happily munch the bitterest of foods.

Cats cannot taste sugar.

More Reliable Than a Laboratory

MAN'S SENSES of sight and hearing are among the best in the animal world. But his sense of smell is not super sharp. Many animals, such as dogs, pigs, deer, and bears, can easily outsmell him.

Yet even with its limited keenness, the human nose does a remarkable job of detecting minute odors. Many odors are so faint they cannot be identified in scientific laboratories. However, our noses are frequently able to recognize these odors in just one or two sniffs. Some odors, of course, are more easily detected than others. Because of their strength and ability to stimulate the odor sense cells, such odors can be smelled when they are present in incredibly small amounts.

Vanillin, a chemical found in the vanilla bean, has a powerful odor of this type. Just a pinch of vanillin placed on a theater stage is powerful enough to send its pleasant aroma as far as the back row.

Outside and Inside the Nose

THE NOSE that points back at us from the mirror is really an outside shell. It protects the delicate mechanism of the inner nose, which does the important job of conveying the air we breathe and smell.

As you breathe, the air is carried over a patch of odor sensory nerves, then into the lungs. The odor sensory nerves — located at

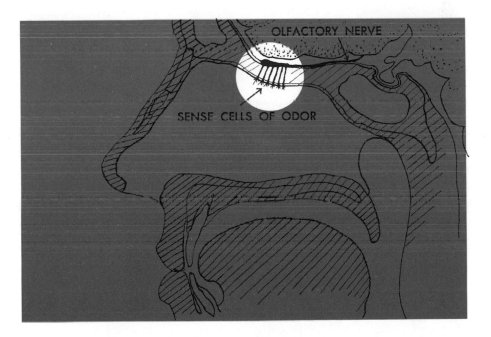

OLFACTORY NERVE

SENSE CELLS OF ODOR

Odors are detected by a patch of sense cells located at the back of the nose.

39

the back of the inner nose — have projections that resemble tiny hairs. When the chemicals in the air touch these projections, an electrical impulse is fired through the olfactory nerve (*see* diagram on previous page). The brain, as in all sense experiences, is the final target. It translates the electrical impulse from the olfactory nerve into a specific smell that may please (steak? flowers?), dismay (garbage? bus fumes?), puzzle (have I smelled that before?), or perhaps not concern us at all.

The Educated Nose

MEN who work with fragrant products, such as tea, coffee, wine, perfume, or tobacco, usually have trained noses capable of identifying a great many odors. The fine differences between these odors are generally confusing or not even noticeable to most of us.

There are tea merchants, for example, who can smell tea leaves and name the exact geographical area where they were grown. An average person can probably distinguish between the smells of six or seven perfumes. Some trained perfume chemists, however, can positively identify over 125 different scents. Doctors, too, have learned to educate their noses, for many diseases can be diagnosed by their smells.

The Japanese have an unusual parlor game that is a competition of noses. High score is achieved by the player who can recognize the greatest number of different odors.

An accurate sense of smell was considered extremely important by the first great scientific detective of fiction, Sherlock Holmes. Once, after he had identified a woman by the scent of her stationery, he pointed out that every criminal investigator should be able to quickly recognize at least 75 different perfumes. But even Holmes

would have been startled at the real-life performance of Ernest Crocker's nose. Mr. Crocker is a trained chemist and perhaps the world's master sniffer. With the aid of his remarkably educated nose, he can identify over 9000 separate odors.

FEELING

THE SENSES of *feeling* are housed in the skin. Unlike hearing or seeing, feeling is not a single sense. It is actually a group of five different senses. These are touch, pressure, heat, cold, and pain. Each of these feeling senses has its own job to perform, has its own reflexes that protect the body from danger, and sends its own messages to the brain.

What the Senses of Touch and Pressure Tell Us

As a SIMPLE experiment in learning how much the feeling senses tell us, touch any object. Almost instantly, without looking or

Figure 12: The Nerves of Feeling

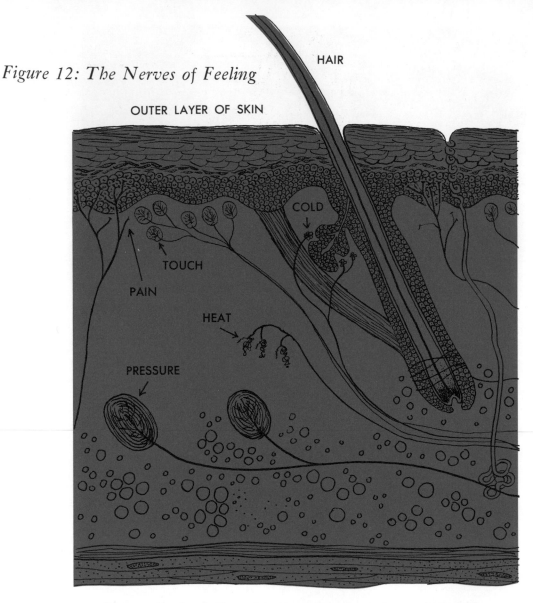

HAIR

OUTER LAYER OF SKIN

COLD

TOUCH

PAIN

HEAT

PRESSURE

Many scientists believe that messages of touch, pressure, heat, cold, and pain are sent to the brain by the nerves shown above. Future research may change this picture or prove it to be accurate.

42

actively thinking, you will know many things about the object. Your senses of touch and pressure will tell you whether it is hard, soft, flat, curved, pointed, solid, mushy, smooth, uneven, or rough.

You use your sense of touch when you pass your fingers lightly over an object. If you push harder with your fingers, you will be using your sense of pressure. Many times we feel things by using the sense of touch and the sense of pressure simultaneously.

With your fingers or other parts of your body, you can tell the difference between a cloth shirt, a leaf, a drinking glass, a mirror, sandpaper, grease, a needle, a pencil, and so on. Almost everything we live with has individual characteristics that we are able to identify through the senses of touch and pressure in our skins.

Should you accidentally touch a sharp object, you will jerk your hand away in a reflex similar to those we previously discussed. Which of the senses triggered off the reflex that protected you from the sharp object? As yet we do not have enough medical knowledge to answer this question fully. Some scientists think, however, that such reflexes are caused by the combined action of three senses: touch, pressure, and pain.

When you hold an electric razor that is operating, the unusual ability of the sense of touch to feel vibrations makes your hand tingle. And, when you lightly run your fingers along the underside of your forearm, you cause tickling, another unusual feeling that is part of our sense of touch.

A rather dull tickle is also felt as you gently brush your fingers across the top of the hair on your forearm or head. Near the bottom of each hair (*see* Figure 12) there is a nerve ending, which is stimulated to fire a message to the brain when the hair is bent.

A great deal still must be learned about the jobs of the other nerve endings of the feeling senses. We do not positively know which

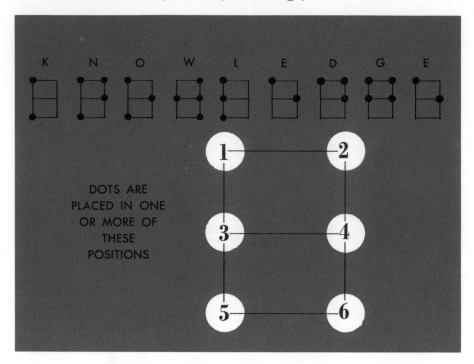

K N O W L E D G E

DOTS ARE
PLACED IN ONE
OR MORE OF
THESE
POSITIONS

1 2

3 4

5 6

Blind people read using the sense of feeling in their fingertips. The alphabet of the blind is called *Braille*. It is made up of one to six dots arranged in different patterns around a tall box. Each dot is raised above the surface of the paper.

The Braille method of reading was invented over 125 years ago by Louis Braille, a Frenchman who became blind at the age of three. Today Braille is read by blind people all over the world.

nerve endings send the actual messages of touch, pressure, heat, cold, and pain through the spinal cord to the brain. Until further discoveries are made, we can only say with accuracy that the messages are sent and that they are received by the brain.

Hot Spots and Cold Spots:
The Senses of Temperature

THE OBJECT that you touched a moment ago may have felt warm or cold, or perhaps there was not a noticeable temperature difference. Heat always flows from a substance that is hot to one that is colder. The temperature senses depends on this flow of heat in and out of the body. When you touch something warmer than your skin, heat flows from it into your body. If the object is colder than your skin, heat leaves the body through the skin and the object becomes warmer.

The skin is a mixture of tiny areas that cover nerve endings. Each of these tiny areas, or *spots,* is sensitive to only one of the feeling senses.

Tap a pencil lightly at different places on your forearm or at the back of your hand. At some spots you will feel a flash of coldness because the cold nerve ending is stimulated. Repeat the tapping, this time using a long nail (with a blunt point) that has been heated in moderately hot water. You will discover many spots where you do not feel the warmth. A feeling of warmth will be felt only on those spots where the hot nerve ending is stimulated.

Occasionally, with careful experimentation, it is possible to touch a cold spot with a warm nail and feel a cold sensation. The opposite, however, does not occur. A hot spot touched with a cold nail does not produce a warm sensation.

In order to find the spots for touch, use a thin hair mounted to the end of a wooden matchstick. The pressure and pain spots are best found with a thin wire.

45

The Unwanted Protection: Pain

PAIN is what we feel when the skin or other parts of the body are hurt. How do we describe this feeling? Sharp, throbbing, dull, itching, steady, biting, piercing — the words themselves are almost painful to read. Every description of pain reminds us that it is the least wanted of the feeling senses. Yet pain, which so often we wish did not exist, is completely necessary to our health.

You are standing in the kitchen. Accidentally your arm touches the hot stove. Your sense of pain sets off a reflex that makes you instantly pull your arm away. If you had not been warned by a painful feeling, your arm might have remained against the stove and been badly burned.

A pain in a tooth, an ear, or anywhere else in the body has a similar meaning. It tells you that an infection or some other danger is present.

Pain is a constant sentinel that warns us of danger either outside or inside our bodies. We know that pain itself does not cause damage to the body. It is the damage that causes the sentinel, pain, to sound its distressing, but protective, alarm.

Scattered Feelings

THE FEELING senses are spread unevenly throughout the skin. The back of the hand, for example, is less sensitive to touch than the fingertips. It is, however, more sensitive to touch than the middle of the back. The soles of the feet and the backs of the elbows are far less sensitive to pain than the cheeks.

One laboratory, using the tapping test, found that in a small area of the neck there are five times more pain spots present than in the same area at the tip of the nose. When the laboratory checked the temperature senses, they learned that the palm of the hand contains less than half the cold spots found in an equal area of the chest. Perhaps their most interesting discovery was that over the entire skin there are many more cold spots than hot spots.

Do These Unusual Senses Exist?

In exploring how the senses of the human body work, we have followed a path of knowledge mapped by many scientists who are in general agreement. It will be interesting to take a short side trip and travel a fascinating but entirely different path — one that leads away from the known senses of the body to the unknown senses that may or may not exist in the mind. Here the directions on the map are no longer clear. For we are entering the area of *extrasensory perception*, where there is much confusion and scientific argument.

Called ESP for short, extrasensory perception is defined as the act of learning something without using the normal senses. Thus whatever is learned is not seen, heard, smelled, tasted, or felt. If ESP exists, it comes to the mind by a method that still has not been explained.

Some universities, like Duke and Harvard, have performed numerous tests to find out whether ESP does exist. There are scientists who feel that these tests have shown that some people definitely have ESP and that others do not. A majority of scientists, however, are not convinced that anybody has ESP. They claim that the results of the tests are not clear and that more proof is needed.

When ESP involves objects, events, or a scene, it is called *clairvoyance*. One famous test for clairvoyance matches the law of chance against a person's ability to guess cards picked from a special deck.

47

There are twenty-five cards in all, each marked with one of five shapes: a star, a plus sign, a wave, a rectangle, and a circle. According to the law of chance, the person taking the test should be able to correctly guess five cards out of the twenty-five. Those who are able to guess more are said to be clairvoyant.

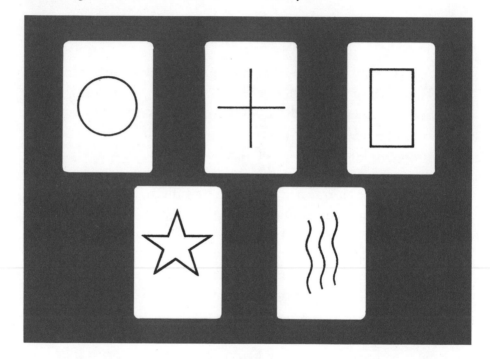

These cards are used to test extrasensory perception. The person being tested tries to guess which shape is on the card that will be turned up next.

Telepathy is another form of ESP. People who are called telepathic are considered to have the ability to know what somebody else is thinking. Scientists who believe in the existence of telepathy say that it cannot be turned on and off at will. In telepathic people, this ability is supposed to occur by itself and without control.

Until more is learned about what goes on in the human mind, the arguments for and against ESP will continue. Does it actually exist? Or are the small group of scientists who accept ESP wrong? These questions can only be answered through further experiments by men of open minds.

THE INNER SENSES

THE HUMAN SENSES we have talked about — sight, hearing, smell, taste, touch, pressure, pain, heat, and cold — relay messages to the brain about events that occur in our environment. They are called *outer senses* because they are stimulated mostly by what is happening outside the body.

We also have *inner senses*, which are stimulated by what takes place inside the body. The inner senses let us know when we are hungry or thirsty, inform us of the position of different parts of the body, and help us to keep our balance.

When You Feel Hunger or Thirst

AN EMPTY stomach demands to be filled. If there is no food in the stomach, it *contracts*, or, draws together. The lack of food also causes a chemical change to take place in the blood. Stimulated both by the contractions and the chemical change in the blood, the sensory nerves in the stomach send signals of hunger to the brain.

Hunger is the condition that exists when our stomachs are truly empty. The desire to eat, however, is frequently caused by *appetite* — a condition of our minds rather than our stomachs. Appetite is a longing for the satisfactions that food can bring, a need to give ourselves some pleasant treat. Hunger forces us to eat almost anything. Appetite leads us — whether our stomachs are full or not — to special foods that our experience tells us we will enjoy.

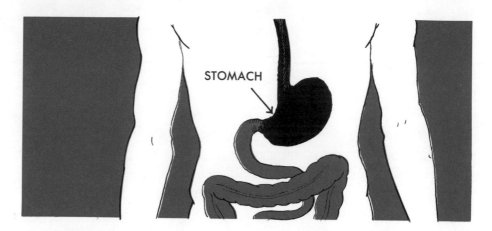

STOMACH

When the stomach is empty, nerves send hunger signals to the brain. It takes three to five hours for food to pass completely through the stomach.

Food is to hunger what water is to thirst. Just as the sense of hunger is stimulated when the stomach is empty, the sense of thirst is stimulated when the linings of the mouth and throat lose water and start to dry out.

Some of the methods by which we lose water are perspiration, normal elimination of body wastes, speaking, breathing warm, dry air, and eating dry or salty food. At times, excitement or nervous strain, such as that felt by many actors before they go on stage, will also create feelings of thirst.

Thus thirst is brought about by different activities of the body and, in some instances, the mind. But whatever the cause of thirst, water provides quick relief.

Water has always been praised by men who were struck with its blessing and its bounty. Salutes to water surely started as many years ago as the human race is old. One writer of the nineteenth century, obviously a man who in his time experienced some powerful thirsts, described water as ". . . beautiful, pure, blessed and glorious, forever the same!"

When you are thirsty, drinking water moistens the mouth and throat, easing their dryness. It also restores a proper fluid level in the rest of the body.

From Walking to Objects in the Dark: The Muscle Sense

ONE OF the most important senses, the *muscle sense*, is also one of the least known. Although the muscle sense guides and informs us of every physical activity of our bodies, it works so quietly we hardly know it exists.

The muscle sense tells the brain where all the parts of the body are and what they are doing. Most of the time this information is received and used by the brain without our awareness.

To learn how the muscle sense works, keep reading and raise your arm over your head. Even though you are not looking at your arm, you will know if it is straight or bent, if your fingers are in a line or positioned separately, and if your wrist is curved or upright.

You receive similar information from the muscle sense when you walk. Because of the muscle sense, you automatically know where your feet and legs are and exactly how they are moving. It is not necessary for you to actually see their position, to watch their motion, or even to think about it.

You use both your muscle sense and your sense of feeling when you find out the shape of an object in the dark. Imagine that you

Music and Sports Require Good Muscle Sense

are in a dark room and that you pick up an object. Almost immediately, without the use of your eyes, you identify the object as a bottle.

How did you know so quickly? First, your sense of feeling told you that it was glass. Then as you moved your hands around the object, your muscle sense told you that your hands had followed the shape of a bottle.

The muscle sense was named some years ago. At that time, it was thought that the brain received signals about the movement and position of the body only from the sensory nerves of the muscles. Later, it was discovered that the tendons and the muscles send signals of the same type. (*Tendons* are tough fibers that connect the muscles to the bones; *joints* are places, such as the knee, where two bones are connected.) Today all three — muscles, tendons, and joints — are considered part of the muscle sense.

TURNING AND TILTING:
THE SENSE OF BALANCE

THE POSITION of your body and of your head are controlled by your sense of balance. Whether you are sitting, walking, standing, running, crouching, or lying down, your ability to keep a steady position is determined by this remarkable inner sense.

We usually think of the ear as the location of the sense of hearing, but the ear also contains the organs of the sense of balance.

Figure 13: The Sense of Balance Is Located in the Inner Ear

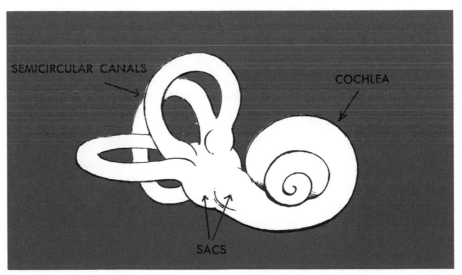

The cochlea is part of the hearing sense. The semicircular canals and the two sacs make up the sense of balance.

These organs are the *semicircular canals* and the two tiny *sacs* (bags), which are next to the cochlea (*see* Figure 13).

The three semicircular canals are curved bony tubes partly filled with a liquid. At the ends of the canals are sensory nerve endings, which have tiny hair cells at their tips. When you turn your head, the liquid moves and pushes against of the hair cells. A message is sent by the hair cells to the brain describing the position the head is in.

The semicircular canals are responsible for a well-known reflex that takes place in accidental falls. If you stumble and fall, the liquid in the canals splashes against the hair cells. Electrical impulses flash through the spine to the hands, which spring out to cushion the fall.

Turning around rapidly is another motion that causes splashing. If the turning continues, the liquid strikes the hair cells with waves of weak and strong stimulations. Dizziness and a confused sense of balance result. The dizziness and confusion disappear after the turning stops and the waves level off.

In addition to the circular motion of turning, we also tilt our heads to the front, to the back, and from side to side. These movements are regulated by the two sacs, shown in Figure 13.

Each sac is filled with liquid and has nerve endings which come together in a patch of tiny hair cells. At the top of each patch of hair cells, there is a tiny "pebble."

The position of the pebble follows the position of the head. If the head is held upright, the pebble pushes straight down on the hair cells. If the head is tilted, however, the pebble shifts and pulls the hair cells in the direction of the tilt.

As the pebble changes position, it stimulates the hair cells, to which it is attached. Electrical impulses are sent by the hair cells through the nerves to the brain. The impulses instantly reveal to the brain the exact position of the head.

THE WORTH OF THE SENSES

THE SENSES have always been an invaluable part of living and learning — helping to make man what he has been in the past, what he is today, and what he may be in the future.

In using the senses to search ourselves and our world, we constantly uncover new wonders and new mysteries. Some of them are clearly and quickly revealed. Others are perplexing and hard to understand. But the difficulties have not halted our progress. For with the help of our senses and our brains, the encyclopedia of human knowledge keeps increasing.

Special Words from the Language of the Senses

Absorbed: taken up, in the way that a blotter absorbs ink. When white light shines on a blue wall, all the colors in the white light, except the blue, are absorbed. The blue is reflected. See *Reflected*.

Axon: the long thread of a nerve along which messages travel.

Cell body: the control center, or headquarters, of a nerve.

Cochlea: a snail-shaped section of the inner ear that contains nerve endings, which are sensitive to sound.

Concave lens: spreads light rays apart. See *Lens*.

Cones: tiny nerve endings located in the retina, which are sensitive to strong light and color. The cones do not work in dim light.

Connecting nerves: act as bridges, carrying messages between other nerves.

Convex lens: bends light rays together. See *Lens*.

Cornea: the tough outer window of the eye.

Dendrites: the group of short threads at the end of a nerve through which messages enter.

56

Extrasensory perception (ESP): the act of learning something without using the normal senses. If extrasensory perception does exist — a question that still has not been satisfactorily answered — it comes to the mind by a method which as yet has not been explained.

Focusing: the ability of a lens to form sharp, clear images.

Frequency: the number of vibrations an object makes per second. Most people can hear sounds with frequencies from 16 to 20,000 vibrations per second.

Illuminated objects: reflect, or bounce back, light to our eyes. Examples: almost everything around us, such as people, trees, books, buildings, animals, furniture, and so on. See *Luminous objects.*

Impulses: short bursts of electricity that are actually messages from the senses to the brain.

Inner senses: are stimulated by what takes place inside the body. They let us know if we are hungry or thirsty, inform us of the position of different parts of the body, and help us to keep our balance.

Iris: the curtain of the eye, which opens and closes to allow more or less light to enter. When we talk of the color of a person's eyes, we are actually describing the irises.

Lens: a curved piece of glass or other transparent material, which bends light rays passing through it.

Luminous objects: give off their own light. Examples: the sun, electric light bulbs, and flames. See *Illuminated objects.*

Motor nerves: deliver orders to different parts of the body, such as the muscles, telling them what to do.

Muscle sense: tells the brain where all the parts of the body are and what they are doing.

Outer senses: relay messages to the brain about events that occur in our environment. These senses are sight, hearing, smell, taste, touch, pressure, pain, heat, and cold.

Overtones: the extra *frequencies* which enrich a tone, making it mellow, fuller, and more pleasant to listen to.

Perceive: to understand. Our ears receive sound waves, but our brains perceive that we are listening to a voice, a bell, a clarinet, etc.

Pitch: the highness or lowness of a sound.

Prism: a solid, three-sided piece of glass that splits light into a brilliant band of rainbow colors.

Pupil: the hole through which all light enters the eye.

Reflected: bounced back. White light is reflected from a white wall. See *Absorbed.*

Reflex: an action in which the muscles of the body move automatically without instructions from the brain. Example: if you touch something hot, the act of instantly pulling your hand back is called a reflex.

Retina: the screen of the eye, which receives the images transmitted by the eye lens.

Rods: tiny nerve endings located in the retina, which are sensitive to dim light. The rods cannot tell colors apart in any light, either bright or dim.

Semicircular canals: curved, bony tubes located in the inner ear, which help us keep our balance.

Senses: those parts of the body, such as the eyes, the ears, and the tongue, which reveal what is happening within us and around us. See *Inner senses* and *Outer senses.*

Sensory nerves: send messages to the brain or to the spinal cord about what is happening inside and outside the body.

Stimulus: anything that causes the sense organs to perform some activity. Examples of stimuli are sound that reaches our ears, light that enters our eyes, and smells that are breathed through our noses.

Synapse: the region where two nerves come together but do not actually touch. The chemical fluids in the synapse transmit messages between the nerves.

Taste buds: tiny regions on the tongue, which house the sense cells of taste.

Vibration: a back and forth movement. Sounds are produced by objects that vibrate.

Index